ROMULUS
AND
REMUS

SUMMER SCHOOL

25 Years of Magical Reading

ALADDIN PAPERBACKS
EST. 1972

First Aladdin Paperbacks Edition, 1997

Aladdin Paperbacks
An imprint of Simon & Schuster Children's Publishing Division
1230 Avenue of the Americas
New York, New York 10020

Also available in a Simon & Schuster Books for Young Readers Edition.

The text of this book is set in Utopia.
Printed and bound in the United States of America.
10 9 8 7 6 5 4 3 2
The Library of Congress has cataloged the Simon & Schuster Books for Young
Readers Edition as follows:
Rockwell, Anne.
Romulus and Remus / by Anne Rockwell.
p. cm. — (A Ready-to-Read book)
Summary: A retelling of the story about Romulus, the legendary founder of
Rome, and his twin brother, Remus, who were raised with wolves.
ISBN 0-689-81291-4 (hc) 0-689-81290-6 (pbk)
1. Romulus, King of Rome—Juvenile literature. 2. Remus (Twin of Romulus,
King of Rome)—Juvenile literature. 3. Roman she-wolf (legendary character)—
Juvenile literature. 4. Mythology, Roman—Juvenile literature.
5. Legends—Rome—Juvenile literature.
[1. Romulus, King of Rome. 2. Remus (Twin of Romulus, King of Rome).
3. Mythology, Roman.] I. Title. II. Series: Ready-to-Read.
BL820.R67R63   1996
398.2'0937'02—dc20   96-25565   CIP   AC

ROMULUS AND REMUS

Written and illustrated by
Anne Rockwell

Ready-to-Read
Aladdin Paperbacks

For Nicholas and Nigel,
James and Daisy

CHAPTER 1

Once there were two baby brothers.

They lived in a forest with their mother.

One was named Romulus.

The other was named Remus.

Romulus and Remus were twins.

They looked almost exactly alike

except for one thing.

Romulus was a little bit

bigger than Remus.

One spring day,
their mother put them in a basket.
She carried it to the River Tiber.
Romulus and Remus slept
in the basket
while their mother
washed clothes in the river.
Snow had melted in the hills.

The water in the river grew higher
and higher and higher.
Soon the water was so high,
it lifted the basket
from the banks of the river.
The basket floated away
with Romulus and Remus asleep inside it.
Their mother didn't see what happened.
She was too busy washing clothes
and drying them in the sunshine.

CHAPTER 2

Romulus and Remus slept and slept
as their basket floated away
like a little boat.
Soon the basket landed with a thump.
It landed far from where
their mother was washing clothes.
Now Romulus and Remus were
too far away
for their mother to find them.

They were under a big fig tree
that grew on a bank
of the River Tiber.

That fig tree was near a high hill
called the Palatine Hill.
A mother wolf lived under the tree.
When their basket landed
with a thump,
Romulus and Remus woke up.
Now they were very hungry!
They were so hungry,
they began to cry.
"Waah! Waah! Waah!"
cried Romulus and Remus.
Romulus cried a little louder
because he was a little bigger.

The mother wolf heard them crying.
She thought they sounded like her
little, furry, hungry wolf cubs.
She knew the baby boys were hungry,
so she fed them.

Romulus and Remus stayed
with the wolf mother
under the big fig tree
that grew by the River Tiber.
They played with
the little furry wolf cubs.

The wolf mother took good care
of them.
She fed them
whenever they were hungry.
The brothers grew big and strong.

CHAPTER 3

Every year, Romulus and Remus
grew bigger.
They were both big,
but Romulus was always a little bigger.
Both boys could run fast,
but Romulus could always
run faster than Remus.
Both boys could jump high,
but Romulus could always
jump higher than Remus.

Romulus and Remus liked to fight.
They would fight with the furry
wolf cubs.
They would fight with each
other, too.
Every time Romulus and
Remus fought,
Romulus won.
And Remus didn't like that.
That made them fight some more.

One day, their wolf mother said,
"Listen, boys!
I have had enough of this.
There will be no more fighting,
Romulus and Remus—do you hear me?"

"Yes, mother," said Romulus.

"Yes, mother," said Remus.

They tried to be good.

Romulus and Remus didn't fight

for more than three weeks.

CHAPTER 4

The years went by.
Romulus and Remus grew up.
They still liked to fight,
but Romulus liked to make
things, too.
Remus liked to run and hunt
more than he liked to make things.

One day they climbed
to the top of the Palatine Hill.
"Look, Remus," said Romulus.
"It is beautiful up here.
We can see very far away.

We can see the River Tiber."

"Yes, that is true," said Remus.

"But now I have seen enough.

Now I want to race you down the hill."

"No," said Romulus.

"Let's build a house
on this hill instead."
And so they did.
It was a beautiful house.

Then Romulus and Remus built
another house.
"I am tired of building houses,"
said Remus.

So he ran down the hill
to where the wolf cubs lived.
They were grown up now,
just like Romulus and Remus.
Remus ran and hunted
with the wolves.
But Romulus went on
building houses.

CHAPTER 5

Romulus built more and more
houses on the Palatine Hill.
When Romulus looked at
the beautiful houses he had built,
he was proud.
"I think I like building
more than fighting," he said.
So he built even more houses.
Romulus built so many houses,
he built a city.
His city grew bigger and bigger.
It was beautiful, too.

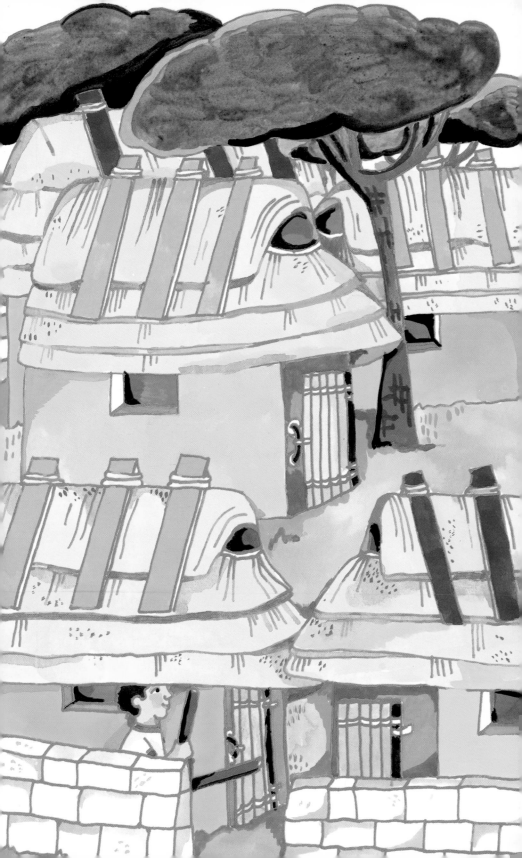

People came from far away to live
in the city on the Palatine Hill.
Most of them were slaves
who had run away from masters
who were mean to them.
They wanted to be free.

Romulus was not mean to them.

He let them be free.

He gave them houses in his city.

Soon more and more people came to live in the big, beautiful city Romulus built on the Palatine Hill. But Remus didn't live in the city. He hunted with the grown-up wolf cubs who lived far away.

"I think my city needs a name!"
Romulus said one day.
"Let me see.
What will I name it?
Well, it is very beautiful.
And it is very big, too.
Just like me."
Romulus was so proud of himself,
he named that big, beautiful city
on the Palatine Hill after himself.
He named it 'Rome' because
Rome started with the letters
R-O-M
just like 'Romulus' did.

CHAPTER 6

"Romulus is big and strong,"
said the people who lived in Rome.
"He builds good, strong houses for us.
He lets us be free,
but he is also very good at fighting.
He can protect us
from people who are mean."
Soon someone said,
"Romulus is as brave
and strong as a wolf.
He built this beautiful city for us.
Why don't we make him our king?"
"That is a very good idea,"
said everyone else.
And so they made Romulus their king.

Romulus was proud to be king
of Rome.
He was happy, too.

Romulus decided to give a party.

He invited Remus.

He invited their wolf mother, too.

Their wolf mother came to the party.

She was very proud of Romulus.

Now he was a king!
She danced with all the people
who lived in the beautiful city
that Romulus built
on the Palatine Hill.

Remus came to the party, too.
Late that night,
he said good-bye to Romulus.
Then he ran down the hill
to hunt with the wolves, far away.